Elite Warriors

AIR COMMANDOS

TOM HEAD

BLACK
RA8BIT
BOOKS

Bolt is published by Black Rabbit Books
P.O. Box 3263, Mankato, Minnesota, 56002.
www.blackrabbitbooks.com
Copyright © 2019 Black Rabbit Books

Marysa Storm, editor; Grant Gould &
Michael Sellner, designers; Omay Ayres,
photo researcher

Library of Congress Cataloging-in-Publication Data
Names: Head, Tom, author.
Title: Air commandos / by Tom Head.
Description: Mankato, Minnesota : Black Rabbit Books, [2019] | Series:
Bolt. Elite warriors | Includes bibliographical references and index. |
Audience: Grades 4-6. | Audience: Ages 9-12.
Identifiers: LCCN 2017027593 (print) | LCCN 2017027694 (ebook) |
ISBN 9781680725414 (ebook) | ISBN 9781680724257 (library binding) |
ISBN 9781680727197 (paperback)
Subjects: LCSH: United States. Air Force–Commando troops–Juvenile
literature. | United States. Air Force Special Operations Command–
Juvenile literature. Classification: LCC UG633 (ebook) | LCC
UG633 .H3798 2019 (print) | DDC 358.4–dc23
LC record available at https://lccn.loc.gov/2017027593

Printed in China. 3/18

Image Credits

CONTENTS

CHAPTER 1

In **ACTION**

It was 2013. A huge storm struck the Philippines. Rain pounded the ground. The wind whipped and howled. Waves washed away houses and cars. The storm left many people homeless and injured. They needed help. The U.S. government sent Air Commandos.

Mission Accomplished

The soldiers jumped to action. The storm had done a lot of damage. But the soldiers knew what to do. They worked with local forces. Together, they cleared places for planes to land. They flew people to safety. They brought supplies and food too.

Who Are the Air Commandos?

Commandos are powerful soldiers. They're part of the Air Force Special Operations Command (AFSOC). These soldiers are always ready for **missions**. They can work anywhere, anytime. Commandos include **pararescuers** and **combat** controllers. They're all highly trained.

AFSOC formed in 1990.

Combat Controllers and Pararescuers

Combat controllers work on the ground with other forces. They are the link between the ground and air. These soldiers guide aircraft and lead attacks.

Pararescuers go on rescue missions. They jump from aircraft into unsafe places. They look for injured or captured soldiers.

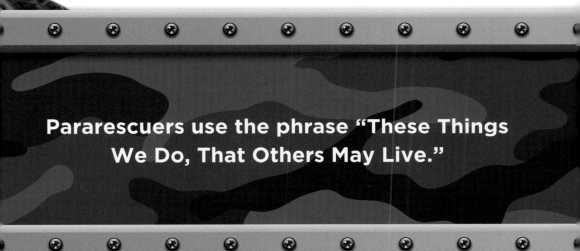

Pararescuers use the phrase "These Things We Do, That Others May Live."

CHAPTER 2

Many Jobs,

Commandos enter enemy land from the sky. They jump from planes. They fast-rope from helicopters. Then Commandos fight. They also study the land. They sneak around and gather information. They then send it back. The information helps to plan other missions.

Commandos often work with other groups.
They need good communication skills.

More than Fighters

Commandos go on many kinds of missions. Sometimes they train **foreign** forces. They teach them how to fight. Other times the soldiers help after natural disasters.

WHERE COMMANDOS HAVE WORKED

These soldiers go on missions around the world.
Here are a few of the places they've worked.

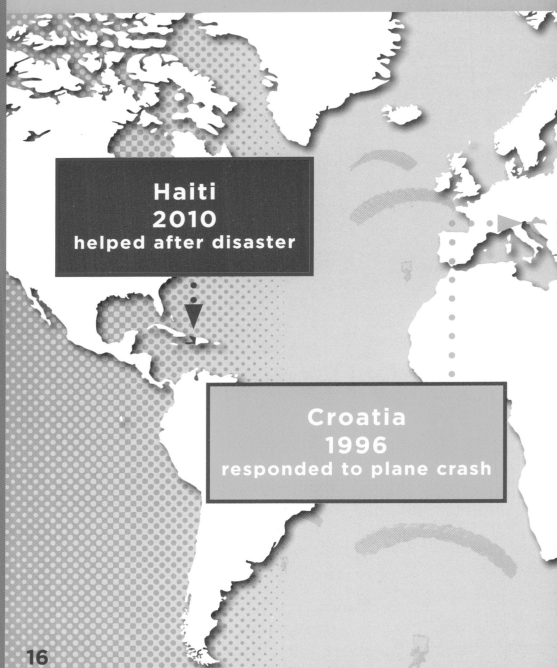

Haiti
2010
helped after disaster

Croatia
1996
responded to plane crash

Iraq
1991
destroyed radar

Afghanistan
2001
performed airstrikes

Philippines
2013
helped after disaster

CHAPTER 3

WEAPONS
and Gear

Commandos need tools to do their jobs. Night-vision goggles let them work in the dark. Radios let them talk to soldiers in the sky. Armor keeps them safe. Commandos also use weapons.

Weapons of the Commandos

rifle

pistol

knife

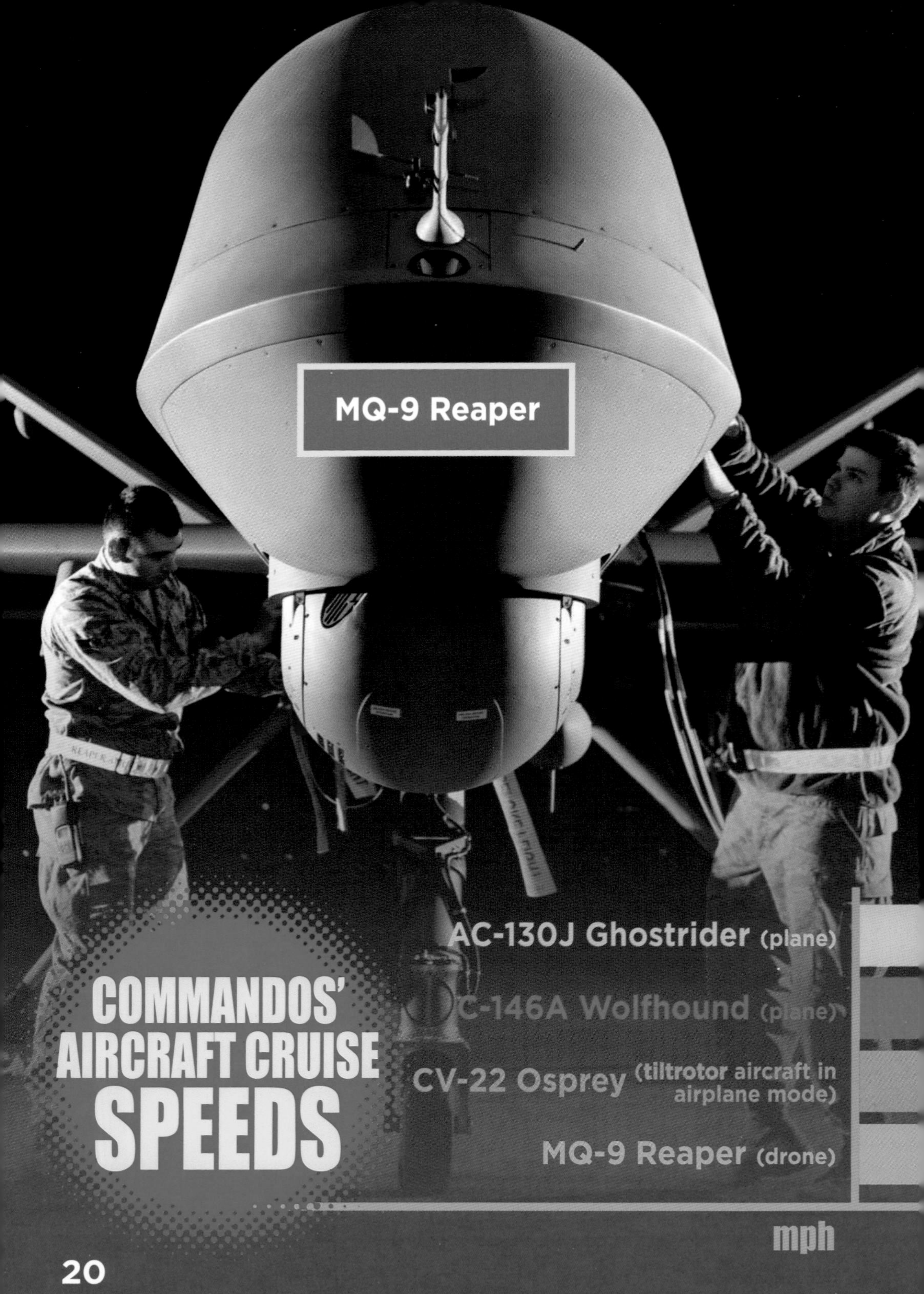

MQ-9 Reaper

COMMANDOS' AIRCRAFT CRUISE SPEEDS

AC-130J Ghostrider (plane)

C-146A Wolfhound (plane)

CV-22 Osprey (tiltrotor aircraft in airplane mode)

MQ-9 Reaper (drone)

mph

Amazing Aircraft

These soldiers use many aircraft too. Sometimes they use choppers. Other times they need planes. In some cases, they might use **drones**.

417 miles per hour (671 kilometers)

311 miles per hour (501 km)

310 miles per hour (499 km)

about 230 miles per hour (370 km)

60   120   180   240   300   360   420

Commandos' Aircraft

BY THE NUMBERS

HEIGHT
39.2 feet
(11.9 meters)

WINGSPAN
132.6 feet
(40.4 m)

LENGTH
97.8 feet
(29.8 m)

AC-130J Ghostrider

HEIGHT
22.1 feet
(6.7 m)

WINGSPAN
84.6 feet
(25.8 m)

LENGTH
57.3 feet
(17.5 m)

CV-22 Osprey

CHAPTER 4

TOUGH Training

Becoming a Commando isn't easy.
Pararescuer training is especially hard.
It lasts about two years. **Recruits** go to
parachutist school. There, they make
at least 30 free fall jumps. Another
part is Basic Survival School. During it,
soldiers learn to survive with little gear.
They also get medical training. They
must be ready for anything.

Recruits Who Pass Pararescue Training

about
20%

BECOMING A COMBAT CONTROLLER

Training takes a lot of time. It is not easy. Soldiers must be tough. They must not give up.

Combat Control Selection Course
2 WEEKS
focuses on basic health and exercises

Combat Control Operator Course
15½ WEEKS
teaches recruits how to become air traffic controllers

U.S. Army Airborne School
3 WEEKS
focuses on parachuting

U.S. Air Force
Basic Survival School
2½ WEEKS
teaches recruits
survival skills

Combat
Control School
13 WEEKS
focuses on combat, land
navigation, and field operations

Special Tactics
Advanced Skills Training
11 TO 12 MONTHS
prepares soldiers for missions

Ready for Anything

Commandos bring airpower down
to earth. They work with other soldiers.
They stop enemies and help those in
need. These soldiers truly are
elite warriors.

combat (kahm-BAT)—active fighting, often in a war

drone (DROHN)—an unmanned aircraft or ship guided by remote control or onboard computer

foreign (FAWR-in)—in a place or country other than the one a person is from

mission (MISH-uhn)—a task or job that someone is given to do

pararescuer (PAR-uh-re-skyo-uhr)—a specially trained person who can parachute to sites and perform search and rescue missions

pistol (PIS-tl)—a small gun whose chamber is part of the barrel

recruit (ri-KROOT)—a newcomer to a group or field of activity

rifle (RI-ful)—a shoulder weapon with grooves in the barrel

tiltrotor (TILT-ROH-ter)—an aircraft that has rotors at the end of each wing which can be oriented vertically for vertical takeoffs and landings, horizontally for forward flight, or to any position in between

BOOKS

Bozzo, Linda. *Air Commandos.* Serving in the Military. Mankato, MN: Amicus High Interest, an imprint of Amicus, 2015.

Freedman, Jeri. *Special Ops: Air Commandos.* Inside Special Ops. New York: Rosen Central, 2015.

Stilwell, Alexander. *Air Force Combat Controllers: What It Takes to Join the Elite.* Military Jobs. New York: Cavendish Square, 2015.

WEBSITES

Air Force Special Operations Command
www.afsoc.af.mil/About-Us/Fact-Sheets/Display/Article/560215/air-commandos/

Air Force Special Ops
www.airforce.com/careers/featured-careers/special-operations

USAF Special Operations
www.americanspecialops.com/usaf-special-operations/

INDEX